Stand & Keep Standing

Gail Grimshaw

Kingdom Publishers

Stand & Keep Standing
Copyright© Gail Grimshaw

All rights reserved. No part of this book may be reproduced in any form by photocopying or any electronic or mechanical means, including information storage or retrieval systems, without permission in writing from both the copyright owner and the publisher of the book. The right of Gail Grimshaw to be identified as the author of this work has been asserted by him/her in accordance with the Copyright, Designs and Patents Act 1988 and any subsequent amendments thereto.
A catalogue record for this book is available from the British Library.

ISBN: 978-1-913247-37-9

1st Edition by Kingdom Publishers
Kingdom Publishers
London, UK.
You can purchase copies of this book from any leading bookstore or email
contact@kingdompublishers.co.uk

CONTENTS

Chapter 1	My Childhood	7
Chapter 2	Our Wedding	15
Chapter 3	My New Family	19
Chapter 4	Life Changes	23
Chapter 5	The Youth Club	26
Chapter 6	Drop In	31
Chapter 7	Different Rules	35
Chapter 8	Answered Prayers	38
Chapter 9	God's Protection	42
Chapter 10	Freedom from the Demons	44
Chapter 11	New Job	46
Chapter 12	Broken Promises	49
Chapter 13	New Beginnings	52
Chapter 14	Prayers and Promises	55
Chapter 15	Ted's Salvation	59
Chapter 16	The Word of God	62
Chapter 17	Still Standing	67

CHAPTER 1

MY CHILDHOOD

Here I am, nine years old, sitting round the table with my family and neighbours, doing the Ouija board.

We had our own homemade board. I am sure a lot of people that we knew had a set of letters and a glass in their cupboard. My neighbour kept hers in a glass cabinet for all to see, it was a regular thing for our family. I would sometimes come home from school, and there would be about six ladies all sitting round the table asking the glass questions, hoping they were going to reach great Aunt Sally, or Cousin Fred. The thing is, the dangers were not known to us, and then we grew up with it as normal, so yes when the glass did move, and it spelt out something, we believed that someone was there. Yes, something was there, but it was not anyone who had died, it was Satan and his demons trying to convince us that this is good, so let's do it again and again! Is it any wonder that so many strange things were always happening in my home where I grew up?

There was often the smell of cigar smoke on the landing upstairs. Once, I saw a hand come around my bedroom door and turn my light off. When I said, "Thank you Dad", he had told me later that he had not been upstairs. Mirrors would seem to attack us that were leaning against a wall, but nothing was moved in front of it. We would go ghost hunting round graveyards. Is it any wonder I was afraid of my own shadow and afraid of the dark? I always slept with the landing light on as I had a small window in my room, so the light shone through. I was always looking behind me scared of what I might see. So many more stories, but I am not going to give the enemy any more of my time.

My childhood was not always a happy one. I did not have a close relationship with my Mother. She never showed any emotion to me, no hugs or affection. I was a modern-day Cinderella and did lots of the cooking and housework. I can remember days when I had to wash the lino in the sitting room, wait for it to dry, then on my hands and knees, I would put polish on the floor. All the time I would have to work around my mum, Nan and three neighbours all sitting drinking tea. She did not want to kiss me, if I went to kiss her goodnight; she would turn her face on the side and put her arm up so I would end up kissing her cheek. I don't know why she was like that, perhaps she did not know herself, but she behaved differently with my two brothers.

People have since told me it sounds like emotional detachment. We all have emotional needs as we are growing up, especially as little girls. Little girls need to feel loved and special. They need to have that love from their parents before they go looking elsewhere for it. All children need to feel confident in them and encouraged to feel that they are special. I did not feel any self-worth, I was not confident in anything that I did other than cleaning and cooking. My family were very negative people; I was always told the negative things about me, never anything good. Because of this, I ended up with a poor feeling of my reflection, each time I looked in the mirror.

A parent's affection shapes their children's lives. Mine lacked affection from my Mum. My dad on the other hand, was more placid, everyone loved my dad. Everywhere we went, someone would call out to him. He was much more easy going. He worked on the railway and was also a chimney sweep. It ran in his family. His dad was a chimney sweep, and when he went away in the First World War, his wife, my Gran took the role over from him. She did not want to give it back when he returned, so she carried on. She was well known as a female sweep; her name was Rosie 'Sooty' Forster. She had eleven children, nine girls and two boys. I have a photo of her going off to clean a chimney and she gave birth to my Auntie the next day. Her picture was displayed in the Imperial War Museum for a while as she was a female chimney sweep during the war. My dad and his brother took on the same role. Sometimes, when my dad had to go and clean a chimney, I went with him to tell him when the brush had gone out through the chimney. He had a push bike with his homemade wheelbarrow on the back where he carried all the chimney brushes and lots of soot. I had his attention and love, but I never felt that with my Mum. When I was young, I used to keep coughing to pretend I was ill, but it didn't make any difference. When I started work, I worked with acid. On my way home from work, I would scrape my knuckles on the wall, so when I went indoors, I thought she would notice me as they were bleeding, but she never did. My boss at work was worried as I had to deal with this acid but thankfully it was okay.

I met Ted when I was fourteen and he was sixteen. I knew then that I only wanted to be with him. We went out with each other for five years, and the whole time my mum made life very hard for us. In those days, the 60's you didn't just leave home and move in with someone, it was classed as sin. It was so different to what it is now. For the five years, we tried our best to keep my mum happy.

She had a lot of rules to keep. For two nights a week we had to stay in, so we never saw each other those days. We never had phones in back then, not even in our houses, so it was very hard maintaining a relationship, but we had to keep to the rules. If we didn't abide by these rules, we would have to stay in for three nights! When I was a little girl, I loved Cinderella and all the Disney stories. I did want my prince to come along and whisk me away on a white horse. Ted didn't have a white horse, but he was my prince who made my life so special. He was so different to what I was used to, he made me feel loved and wanted. Yes, my Prince did come along.

Ted and I met when we were young teenagers. I used to get on an early bus to school just to see him pay his fare then go upstairs. We both used to go to a dance at the weekends at a place called The Paget. It was a great place, lots of music and live bands. Many nights we enjoyed ourselves with good music. Ted worked with my cousin, so one Sunday we all met at a coffee shop called Dimascio's. That was another good place to meet up in the sixties so there we met, and Ted walked me home. He asked me if I would like to go on a coach trip to Margate that his Auntie had organised. Off we went. Margate was our first date and we returned there many times even when we had our three sons, we would go off on the train with our bags packed and with all that we needed for the day.

Margate was the well-known place in the sixties for mods, rockers and Dreamland. I remember one trip we were there in the sixties; we were sitting up in the café which was up one end of the front by the clock tower. We watched as the mods and rockers were fighting on Margate beach. The beach used to be very busy in those days. We later found out that Teds Mum and Dad had met in Margate and lived there for a while. It meant a lot to us in the early days. It was special to us and we went there many times. We loved the scenic railway in Dreamland. The sixties were so exciting with so much to do. We did not have much money, but we had so much fun. Each year we would go to Wembley to see the New Musical Express show through a coach trip. There were so many big bands and singers there. Most days you would see The Beatles, The Rolling Stones, The Who, or Small Faces. We loved that show and we looked forward to it each year. You could see so many good bands with only one ticket. Each concert would run for nearly four hours, and we went for about six years running. We also spent a lot of time in a coffee bar in Herne Bay called Macaris. In the sixties, a lot of Italian coffee bars started up everywhere. We did not drink much coffee in those days it was all tea. The coffee bars were well known for bringing in Frothy Coffee which now is called latte. In Macaris, we used to have a Knickerbocker glory between us as we could only afford to share one.

On one side of my life, I was very happy, and so in love. On the other side, I was so sad as my Mum did not like Ted at all. Mainly because she did not choose him, I did. He was so polite to her and good to me, but it was not enough for my mum. I don't know why my mum treated me like she did. As a teenager, I felt invisible to her, lonely and unloved. That is why I think the depression came along, which in the 60's wasn't really recognised or talked about. That's why each time I went to the doctors, he was already writing out a prescription for my new medicine. I never knew what it was called but all I remembered was the taste, and it was yellow.

Emotional detachment wasn't recognised in those days as they are now. Perhaps a lot of people like me could have had a loving relationship with their mums instead of always trying to get attention and love. I was never allowed to show my feelings if I started to cry. Mum would tell me to go upstairs to my bedroom and not to cry in front of her. My pillow became my best friend, even when someone who was special died; I still had to hold onto my pillow as I was still told the same thing. It became a part of me that I thought I was doing wrong and I told myself not to cry in front of people to keep myself safe. Years later when I became a Christian, I had gone to see Suzzette Hattingh. She was a well-known evangelist. I had gone forward for prayer at the meeting, and as soon as she laid hands on me, I was out in the spirit. I can remember Suzzette saying over me, "The Lord said that you have kept too many tears inside of you so cry them out". Now she didn't know me, so I knew it was from God. I cried on and off for the next two days. We talk a lot about Mirror Image. A daughter will look at her mum and try to reflect that same image as she grows up. A daughter should be valued and loved for who she is with unconditional love, but I never knew love. From that moment, I struggled with my self-image and my emotions. Mum couldn't show emotions to me as she was very negative about the way I looked and the things I did. One day I was getting ready for school, I was about 15, and she said you're not going to school today; you're going to the hospital to see a doctor. The doctor turned out to be a psychiatrist, and she had made the appointment.

I went on the bus with my dad, my mum never came with me and she didn't even talk about it. When I walked in the building, I felt so out of place with so many people just sitting there walking up and down. Some were banging their heads against the wall; I was so afraid.

I was called in and had to speak to a female doctor, who held my hands out to see if I was shaking. She asked me a lot of questions. After I came out of the room, she called my dad in to speak to him. On the way home on the bus I asked dad what she said, all he told me was that I didn't get on with my mother. Mum never asked me how I got on at the doctors when I arrived home and she never mentioned it to me. It was as if it never happened. Not many people knew that it did, especially the rest of my family. I just carried on and I remembered one day when I was 15, I had come home from school. I always cooked a casserole for dinner on Wednesdays and had mixed it altogether. Mum was in the sitting room next to the kitchen. When I went to light the oven with a match, it blew up. Mum had left the gas on so it just exploded. My hair was on fire, plus my eyebrows and lashes had all gone.

Thankfully my dad had heard the bang and came running in from the garden and threw a towel over my head. I was in shock but all I got was, "Now look what you have done to your mum, you've upset her". I had just come in from school, but it was me who got the blame. One night, mum said "You're not going out tonight", for no reason. Ted didn't know until he came up for me. I was so frustrated I ran upstairs and somehow; I had the strength to move all my furniture and barricade myself in my room. I was crying so much that I could not control myself. My neighbours on both sides had knocked the door to tell mum and dad that they could hear me sobbing so much and asked if I was okay. I stayed there all night and no one spoke to me. I was alone and broken, I just needed some calm and peace in my life. The arguments just went on and on. I come from an era where we had a lot of rules that we had to go by and to be honest it didn't do us any harm, but my Mum's rules were an exception. We respected our parents; we were afraid of the police and we must do what our teachers told us to do. Girls were afraid to get pregnant because if you did, the only help you got was from your parents. That is why so many girls had to have the babies adopted because they had no means of keeping them. You didn't get money from the Social Services in those days, so you were on your own. There wasn't the birth control that there is now, to stop you getting pregnant. Abortions were not the answer, especially backstreet clinics, so there was a lot of babies born out of wedlock. This is a saying no one uses anymore. If you lived together before you were married it was called living in sin and having sex before you were married was fornication so there was a lot of difference in the 50s and 60s. I can remember it was found out that one of my neighbours who had four children had never been married, that was the talk of the street for a long time. Most teenagers left school at 15 and went straight out to work, we didn't have the chances of education like they do now, and most young people stayed living at home until there were married or enrolling into any of the services. We never had holidays abroad as it was only for the rich. Our holiday meant living in a little hut down, hop picking in Chilham for the summer holidays.

These were the happiest memories of my childhood. All the families that went from my road travelled down in the back of a lorry to Selling or Chilham, with not much luggage at all. All we needed were a few clothes. We did not have the amount of clothes that young people have now, and we had nothing like wet wipes or spray bleach! We would pick the hops all morning, and then eat our sandwiches with hop stained hands.

Those days were wonderful. All we had was a tilly lamp in a little hut and the beds were made of straw. We spent evenings in the cook hut singing all the old songs, and the kids would swap comics to look at in bed if the light was strong enough. My dad would come down at weekends and all the children at the camp used to knock our hut door and ask if was going to take them out. He was very popular with them. We would all follow him round the farm and along the woods. We would have to stop and listen to a bird singing and tell him what it was. He was very good with birds he was always right. We always wanted to tell him the right answer. He always had his mouth organ with him, so the evenings were spent down in the cook hut with the fires going and Dad playing the old songs. Everyone joined in as they all loved him.

Hop picking was fun, and we spent a wonderful time out in the country, everyone joining together. In Kent, we did all the fruit and vegetable picking. We would earn money while also being out in the open throughout the summer; I don't remember it ever raining in those summer days whilst working on the farms. I had gone pea-picking with my Mum when I was only two months pregnant with David. It wasn't so bad at first but as we had worked our way up further in the field, I was exhausted as I had to carry each big basket back to the tractor to be weighed. I also had to carry my Mums as well. As I was waiting for the basket to be weighed one of the ladies had told me she was pregnant. She then told me that is why she was doing the pea picking to lose the baby she was expecting. That was it, when I told Ted that night he said no more, we wanted our baby, so I never went back. The last time I went bean picking was when I was expecting Lee. I had gone with my sister-in-law. David, Darren and their cousin enjoyed it as they were free in the fields. They just ran around and had fun all day while we picked the beans. One day when it started to rain, I remember the farmer's wife called us into the barn to keep dry and she gave us hot soup. I loved the field work and in Kent there was a lot of it. They were fun days. I wish that children today could know that joy. No phones, electric or social media, just happiness at making games and all being together. My last time of hop-picking came was when I was 14, I just went for the days at Rainham. I cried buckets when the machines took over, I always tried to show Ted and my sons where we were in Chilham but I could never find it.

CHAPTER 2

OUR WEDDING

My dad worked on the railway, so we had access to cheap tickets. In the summer, we would travel up and down to Margate and various other places. Not many people had cars in those days, especially in my road, so my Nan used to arrange coach outings to Margate with all the families in our road. We would all sit in a half circle on the beach and have a lunch that we would have put together, and then we would play games on the beach like Rounders etc. They were fun days, but once people started getting cars, the outings stopped People were going out in their own time. The same thing happened with Christmas parties my Nan used to arrange. We used to take all the food and crockery over in the prams as no one had a car. We used to have to paint the cups and saucers underneath, so we knew who they belonged to. We didn't have alcohol, just cups of tea and orange juice. If any of the men wanted a beer, they would go in the pub opposite the hall, but not for long as we were dancing and there were games going on in the hall. Sounds strange now, but they were good times.

Ted and I had been going out together for five years before we could get married. I was too young, but we were so in love. I just wanted to be with him all the time, he was so good looking and a good football player. I used to go and watch him play, and cheer him on, even when I was freezing cold. The best quality Ted possessed for me was that he was a strong man. I had grown up with a loving dad, but he was so weak. When decisions had to be made, he only sided the way that my mum would choose, even if you didn't agree with her. I remember the night when Ted came up to see mum and dad to ask if we could get engaged. Mum just sat there, clicking on her knitting needles, without even looking at us. Without any answer, she just cut him off. We walked out the front door, I was in tears, and dad came running out and said, "I would give you my blessings, but I have to go along with what mum says". I cried out to him, "Why couldn't you say that in front of mum?" He was too scared to speak. Yes, Ted was that prince I had waited for, and I knew he would never let anything or anyone hurt me. I felt so safe with him and I had never felt that before.

We had our engagement. We went to Canterbury for the day to buy my ring. When we came home, I went to mum to show her, and again she just ignored me. We had a little party over the Cricketers pub near where Ted lives with some close friends, and my auntie, but mum never came. I would come home from work and an argument would begin. My mum would say "You're staying in tonight". Now, as we didn't have phones in those days, Ted would walk up to pick me up, not knowing, only to be told I wasn't allowed out.

I had a neighbour, an older lady called Bennett. She loved me, and she knew me from the day I was born. She was at my birth. She had lost her only daughter at eight months old, so I think she loved me as if I was her own. She also loved Ted. She would come out of her house and take Ted indoors, as he was upset. He had asked, if he could speak to me, but my mums answer was always no. My mum would not let us see each other at all. I think she thought Ted would get fed up with her strictness, but she underestimated how much we loved each other. Sometimes, I wondered how Ted survived so much trouble, but it was because he loved me. He was a good person. On Sundays, he would come up after dinner to pick me up to go for walk or to the cinema, we didn't have cars in those days, so we walked everywhere. Ted was always wearing his suit, shirt and tie. In the 60's, you always dressed up on a Sunday. He always looked smart. One Sunday, he was due to pick me up, and over the Sunday dinner an argument started once again as it did over many meal times. I was so frustrated that in the end I threw my knife and fork down and ran out of the house, without a coat, money or anything. I just ran. I first went to a local cemetery where I sat for a long time crying. I always felt so comfortable there, I suppose because it was so quiet with just the birds singing. I just wanted some peace in my life. I kept walking all over Gillingham from the bottom to the top, but at least five hours crying, and broken, I eventually went to Ted's house. He was frantic because all he thought was, I had given him up. When he had turned up at my house, my mum had told him that I had gone out but he could see my coat was still on the hook. He thought I did not want to see him. He took me home at about 10:15pm, and not a word was spoken when I got home. I had run out of the door about 1:30pm crying, and yet here I was at 10:15pm and not even an "Are you okay?"

That was sadly how life was for most of the five years, and that was why I ended up on medicine from the doctor for my nerves. I didn't know what it was called, but on a really bad day, I would go in the bathroom and just drink it, not a spoonful, but straight from the bottle. I just wanted to feel happy at home. When I was sixteen, it must have been another row, and my mum wasn't speaking to me. Each place I went to, she would leave the present boxes around, no happy birthday, just presents. I was so worn out with the arguments; I just wanted them to stop. I did a lot of chores in the home; I cooked on my day off from work, cleaned the house and did the washing.

In those days, it was normal to bring the old copper boiler from the shed, up some concrete steps and then do all the whites once a week. It was a very hard job putting out hot sheets from a copper boiler into the sink, but I did it. When we made our wedding arrangements, we didn't have much money, but we had a proper church wedding in the Methodist Church and a party in the local hall. There wasn't any joy with the arranging at home. One day, my mum had been out. When she returned, she threw a parcel at me and said, "Here is your wedding dress material", and went out to the kitchen. Thankfully, it was beautiful, just plain material, it but shone like a pearl, and I loved it. As Mum was good at sewing, she made my wedding dress, and my three bridesmaid dresses. She did the machining, and I helped with the accessories. There were lots of flowers to sew on to get the result.

Sadly, the rows were still going on, daily. Sometimes, we would sit up until two in the morning, arguing about the same thing. I had to get up to go to work the next day! The rows continued and I was just so worn out with the arguing. I wanted to look forward to my wedding plans, but I reached the point where I just wanted it to be over as I thought the rows would stop. I did not realise that in some way they just got worse. The night before Ted and I were married, my mum's last words to me were, "I suppose I will never see you again". They were not good words to go on my honeymoon with; I had to focus on the next day, my wedding day.

CHAPTER 3

MY NEW FAMILY

I was getting married to the love of my life, and we were going to start a new life together. We stayed in Tidworth for a few days for our honeymoon, in my brother's house as he was away. We could not afford to go away anywhere but we had each other, and that was all we needed. We had been let down on a rented house. We were all set to take the house on, but someone had come along and paid a cash offer to the estate agent. We had to take what was available. In the end, we ended up in a flat above a shop which I hated. It was a food shop, and when it was hot, the smell of the vegetables was horrible. I fell pregnant straight away with David. We were so happy as we just wanted to have a family of our own. We were walking on cloud nine.

When I was six weeks pregnant, I told my parents after my check up at the doctors that I was having a baby. I was so happy, but mum was staying at my brothers in Tidworth at that time, so I was going up to my dad's house, cooking and making sure he and my brother were okay. One day I asked if mum had written and he said yes but he couldn't show me the letter. I asked him why, and he told me she was so upset that I was pregnant and wanted to finish her life, so he never let me see the letter.

I had done the right thing, got married then got pregnant, which was important in those days to do it that way round, but still she wasn't happy. The flat we lived in was very damp, and as time went on, it became worse. Just before Christmas, we moved into my Mum and Dad's house just to tide us over, but it ended up being a year. It was a bad mistake, Ted hated it. We would walk the streets looking for somewhere to live but when they saw we had a baby; they were not interested. It became harder and there was more pressure on me and Ted. One of

Ted's football friends was selling his house, so we investigated it. We didn't have any money, but somehow, we managed to get a hundred percentage mortgage, so when David was a year old, we moved into our own home. What bliss! We only had two or three pounds to our name, but we had a home that was ours. The house needed a lot of work to be done to it but Ted was so clever, he could put his hand to anything, and it was always good, as he was a perfectionist. In those days people had what they were given, when they got married. I had never heard of a wedding present list. We ended up with our kitchen having three different colours, red, blue and yellow table and chairs and cupboards deep blue.

It stayed like that until we could afford to buy new tins of paint and kitchen furniture, but we had our own home and that was so important to us. Ted made so many fitted cupboards in the bedrooms, and completely fitted our kitchen within a few years of us moving in. I can remember walking on a couple of floorboards for a while, while he worked in the kitchen as he could only work on it at weekends and evenings, but it was so worth it. He worked all the overtime he could, and we made it our home comfortable and homely. We were so happy.

In 1971, Darren came along. We were so blessed with our family, and that was when I met Carole my neighbour. She also had a son, so we got on really well. We became such good friends and shared a lot of times with the children. In 1974, Lee came along and I remember the nurse saying in hospital, "You must be so proud to have three sons", and yes, we were.

We did so much together, and our house was a happy home. However, the battles were ongoing with my Mum. Before Lee was born, my mum had fallen out with me once again. She was jealous of my friendship with Carole, so she hadn't been around for some time. This happened regularly. She never came around when Lee was born, so she never really got to know him until he was 14 months old, she had then sent a message and asked if me and the boys would go to Windsor Castle with her and Dad. I agreed to go.

Deep down I wanted her to see what a precious family I had, and what she had been missing, it was strange as we went up to London on the train but she did not really know anything about Lee, as she had not seen him. David and Darren must have looked different as it was well over a year since she had seen them. She never came when we had Lee christened. Mum and Dad were invited and all the family but only one of my brothers came. One stayed away, but his wife came in after the service started and sat in the back of the church. I loved and respected her for that for choosing to do what she wanted, not what she was told to do. They all missed out on such a lot when my children were young.

Life was good for us as a family, we never had a lot of money, but we were so happy. We loved the time with the boys. We had all what we'd asked for, and used to go up the woods, and take a picnic wherever we were going. We just loved being out with them. When we had our dog to join the family, we were out more than ever, no matter what the weather, she was a border collie called Jessie, and she loved the snow. When Ted and the boys went to the field to play football, Jessie went in goal. When it snowed, Jessie would love to be out in it. We used to go up the Darland Banks near our home with a sledge that Ted had made for the boys. It was a steep hill to slide down, but we all had turns on it. Jessie used to run down chasing us on the way down, jumping all over us when we landed safely at the bottom of the slope. At the same place when the boys were young, Jessie sat still when we told her to, and the boys would go off and hide in the woods. Ted then would say to her, "Go and find the boys, Jessie". Off she would go, jumping all over them and then come running back to me and Ted, looking back, barking, as if to say, "Come I will show you where they are." She adored the boys, and she always went with them when they went out to the woods.

We had a holiday on our own with the boys in the Isle of Wight. We had so much fun. It was our first real holiday, but deep down when I was on my own, I was still afraid of so many things, especially the dark. When the boys were young, I would leave the landing light on. This was really to help me, because I was afraid to go to sleep without it. When they got to the age when they didn't need it, I kept trying to find a reason to leave it on. I now know it stemmed from what I did, calling up the dead. When you play in Satan's camp, he does not like to let you go. I didn't even let Ted know about my fear of the dark, I was afraid I saw shadows when the light went off. I grew up with many strange things happening in my parent's house, but that was where we did the Ouija board, so yes it was expected when you mess around in the enemy's camp.

In 1980, Carole my neighbour had suddenly gone to a meeting that was happening in our town to hear a Christian speaker talk about accepting Jesus as your Saviour. He was also laying hands on people and asking Jesus to heal them. It was very new to me; she went along and became a Christian that night, asking Jesus into her life. I did not like the change in her at all, she wanted to introduce me to Jesus, but I said I was already a Christian. I had been brought up in a Methodist church so I thought, "How can she tell me what I already know?" She told me about being born again, so I thought I would look this up when I was on my own to see if it was true. I had no idea where to look in my Bible. It had collected dust on a shelf for a long time. I didn't know if it was in the old or New Testament, but I opened up my Bible, and there it was on the very page,

"Very truly I say unto you, no-one can see the Kingdom of God unless they are born again." (John Chapter 3, Verse 3)

How wonderful God works, of all the pages that could have opened up to, it was the right page for me. Praise God! But I still carried on trying to fight it. Carole had invited me to a ladies Christian meeting. Wow! I thought at first, they are all too nice. In those days, there were a lot of small Christian books (tracts) left around telling you all about the sinner's prayer. When Carole went off to the toilet I quickly put some tracts in my handbag before she came back, I did not want her to think I was interested. Each time I was searching, and finally Carole invited me and Ted along to a meeting where they would be praying for healing. Everything was so new to me, I had never experienced this in my Methodist church that I grew up in, so it was a different way of life, but I embraced it all, and it soon became a way of life for me. We took Teds mum along with us. It was there I truly met with Jesus. He revealed himself to me and became my Lord and Saviour, changing my perspective completely, what a new way of living for me! This was in 1980, I didn't have a big explosion or thunderclap, but all I can say is that it was like God had opened the curtains, and I was seeing a brand-new world in front of me. It was so different than my old life.

CHAPTER 4

LIFE CHANGES

Here I was, a new Christian with so many changes going on in my life. There was so much to take in, I had been on medicine for my nerves for a very long time since I was a young girl, with no one trying to find out why, but within a few days from accepting Jesus, I just stopped and threw the medicine away, even though no-one had told me to. When I gave my life to Jesus, everything changed. My dad had started going to a spiritualist church and kept asking me to go with him. I can remember one day, my dad had picked up a book in my home that was about someone who had been a spiritualist but had then found Jesus as her Saviour. My dad was enticed by the front cover of the book, and picked it up and said, "I will borrow that to read". I remember at that moment I felt slightly nervous, as I knew the story, I had read it.

A few days later, he came in like thunderclap and threw the book at me; hitting me in the face, and shouted "Don't you ever give me a book like that again." I probably knew I would get a bad reaction but perhaps that was the start of his wanting to disown me. I had found my one true God and I was so happy. I was trusting God for so many things, even Ted did not understand the change in me, and he did not want to understand, but he loved me, so we lived through it. He did not understand why I wanted to go to church each week; he did not want to come. By that time, the boys were coming along too, and I think he felt left out, but did not want to come with us. He realised something was different but could not understand it. Around that time, Ted had his wages stolen at work. In those days people were paid in cash each week, usually a Friday. We were desperate; we had three growing boys to feed and no savings. I had gone to church on the Sunday and after the service a lady came over to me and handed me an envelope and said, "God said I should give you this". In the envelope was forty pounds which was the exact amount that I had in those days to buy the food for the week. No one new about the money that had been stolen, but God knew. How wonderful that He looks after us.

In 1982, my parents and family were in my home on Easter Sunday when suddenly, they all walked out and said they were not coming back. I had laid out food for everyone as it was Lee's birthday as well, but all nine of them went, and that was the very last time they spoke to me or my family. In the space of one day, I had lost my mum, dad, two brothers, my two sisters-in-law, two nephews and one niece. Additional to this, all these years later they have grown up and had families of their own, but I don't even know them. I could not understand why they did not want anything to do with my sons as they were their grandchildren, but I suppose it was because of me. Sometime after that my dad had ignored Lee in the alley as he was taking my brothers son to school, the same school that Lee went to. Lee had said, "Hello Grandad", but my dad ignored him. He was only eight years old,

The long process of disowning and rejecting me and my family had begun, and it lasted until their deaths eleven years later. Each Christmas I used to think that year they would come to see us, but they never did. I used to get tearful each time I heard, "Have yourself a merry little Christmas", as it just reminded me of their rejection, not only me, but all my family. I had heard lots of nasty and hurtful things that had been said about me, which hurt very much. They called me a religious maniac! They called me names and had said some really bad things about the youth club Carole and I later ran. I was told that mum was even going to tell my pastor at the time that I was up to no good. Some of the people from her church had ignored me because they had believed the things they had heard, yet they had known me since I was five years old, when I started in their church. I could not keep fighting the lies that had been said. When my mum died Ted went to the funeral to represent our family as they made it clear they did not want me there. The same thing happened when my dad died. At my mum's funeral the vicar said my mum only had two sons, nothing about a daughter, so I had been so left out from their lives. I had written to my mum and asked her to forgive me for whatever it was that I had done, but she never replied; I knew she had received it as my Auntie had told me. I also had written to one of my brothers the same letter but again no answer. No one has ever actually told me why they all walked out on me in 1982, I just assumed it was because I had become a Christian, but my Mum was going to the Methodist church so I could not understand. Friends had told me that she had called me names, so they did not understand my love for Jesus. It was so sad as I was actually very happy, but my family did not want to understand. It is so sad that I had found a true love through Jesus but to my family it seemed to be wrong.

CHAPTER 5

THE YOUTH CLUB

In 1982, I had been praying, "Lord, what can I do for you?" Carole and I got together and prayed about it, and God spoke to both of us separately, and said we should start a youth club called Gillingham Christian Youth Club. It was born! We contacted the local council, and someone came to see us. He said we would have to function under the rules of the council, so we told him, "No, we come under Gods rules, and we will run it as God wants it to be run". He went away with a grin on his face and probably thought we were insane.

We started in a friend's front room, she was a lovely Christian lady who lived on her own and was willing to give her room to us once a week. She was very special with a great love for God and a great love for the young people too. She was a great prayer warrior and she prayed always for the Youth Club. She was a strong woman of God.

We really relied on our children and their friends for the first week, as we never advertised or sent out any flyers. In fact, for the whole six years, we never advertised, we just trusted whoever turned up God wanted there whether it was five or fifty people. The first week, there were about fifteen, then it grew and grew until there were so many, we needed somewhere bigger like a hall to fit them all in. They were good days; it was where we began. God's protection was always with us. One boy had been bad, so we banned him. We had a three week ban rule, and then they could come back. He took it badly and wanted to pay us back, so he had arranged for some of his older friends to pay us a visit when the youth club was on to roughen the place up. That evening, we had started, and there was a knock on the door. There were older, angry-looking young men standing there. We kept calm and said, "Oh, you have missed the beginning of the talk, but if you want we can start again. To our shock they came in and listened to what we had to say, although they argued a lot about it, but they stayed all evening, and some came back for weeks after.

The boy who had sent them, phoned up later expecting to hear the worse but instead they enjoyed the debate we had about God. We found out what was intended of them that night, but God is so faithful. One early Sunday morning, I had the police at my door wanting to know of friends of one of the boys as he was missing. I said, "Surely his parents knew them", but they did not that is why they sent us to you. He was later found lying in a gutter somewhere high as a kite. Another week, the Youth Club attendees had gone home, and we used to have a cup of coffee while we helped clear up. There was a frantic knock on the door and one of the girls said, "You have to come quick as a lot of our boys had gone to the local fish and chip shop, and outside were a crowd of youths with knives waiting for our youth club boys to come out". The owner of the shop had told them they have to leave as he was worried it would be damage to his shop. We went straight away but we did not want them to look weak, so we just waded right through the knife-wielding crowd and said, "Oh, you've got the chips then". It was almost like the crowd outside frozen in time. They looked like statues and unable to move knives in their hands. What an amazing God we serve.

In those days there were always problems with the two towns that were close to each other. There was always trouble, and especially as our youth all wore parkas and flight jackets, most had Vespa's or Lambretta's, so they didn't go down very well with a lot of other youths. A few times they were in dangerous positions, they prayed, and all was well, but I still think they were always in awe at what God did to keep them out of trouble. When the youth club got bigger, we had to find a hall as there were too many for the front room, although we were always thankful as many a life was changed in that room. We were offered a hall down the road from us and soon the car park was getting full of scooters. We loved all of them, even though it was hard to cater for all sometimes. Carole and I used to go out to a special Christian shop in Bromley every so often and buy tracts and books. We used to buy small American chick books which were at that time very helpful. They were very useful for the youth club as they were short stories with a real message, and some very graphic images. They loved those books. One time, we had come back from Bromley with quite a few and spread them around the hall when the youth club had finished. We found some of the club had ripped the paperwork up and when we checked the loos before leaving, we found the urinals blocked with the tracts, and some other pretty unpleasant things which we had to clear out. Talk about getting your hands dirty! I was angry that they had done that, but we always must get over it and carry on and forgive them.

Some weeks, some of the men from the church wanted to come and speak to them, but the boys didn't take to outsiders. One week, one of the young men came in, and we had to stop one of the boys. He was just about to throw a chair over his head, and that night he wasn't happy as some of the boys had put chewing gum in his hair. He was a very well-dressed guy, so he went off home and he never came back. We had two young men who have just been released from a prison that wasn't very far away to us. We had just started visiting this prison with a group to attend the Sunday morning service with them, and these two men wanted to come and speak to the youth club when they were released. They turned up at the club, and we went out to meet them. When they walked up to the steps, suddenly, the door opened, and they caught a glimpse inside, and both were afraid to go in. Considering they have just been released from prison, I thought they would be able to take it, but they saw fear where we did not. That's why God chose two ordinary women to love them, whoever came in the door. We had tables and chairs scattered around the hall and we had to go around and check as some of the boys had knives on them and they were carving out things in on the table. We took the knives away from them and told them they would be locked up in the kitchen and they could have them back when they left. One week they came in with long 6-inch nails. They were going around digging them in each other. Once again, we took them away. One of the boys had gone around the back and broke into the kitchen to get his knife back, but we found out and we stopped him.

Our Father told us what was going on many times when they came in. We would be writing down their names in the book. I said to one boy, "I want that knife that's in your pocket please", and he said, "How do you know I have a knife. Have you got eyes in the back of your head?" Jesus took care of everything; we never felt scared or threatened with any of them, just pure love. Thank you, Jesus.

When we took names to put in our attendee book, they never gave us their real names. Most weeks, we had about fifteen Paul Wellers and so many Roger Daltreys. For a long time, we were getting fifty young men, we had a few girls, but at that time, it was mostly boys. How we love them. Sometimes some of them were trouble, and I remembered one boy had been running across the Bowling Green, and one of the members complained and wanted us out. We had to go to a meeting with the man in charge and the man who made the complaint. He was a long-time member at the club. We prayed hard as we did not want to find another place, we prayed so hard and went down to the meeting. God had given us the scripture which was in the living bible and it was;

"The Lord my God is my fortress - the mighty Rock where I can hide. God has laid the sins of evil men to boomerang upon them. He will destroy them by their own plans are God will cut them off." **(Psalms 94: 22 and 23)**

We prayed that prayer and claimed the promise. The man in charge then said, "No. These ladies will continue as they are helping the community". The complaint backfired, thank you Jesus.

One week, the youth club all started coming in and one of them rushed to say, "One of the girls on the way had been beaten up, and was lying on the ground, and she was unconscious". The ambulance was called, and the police turned up. They asked us a lot of questions, but we couldn't really help them with information. Once they had gone, the youth club just went off to find who did it with cricket bats and clubs. They were so mad that someone did that to their friend. We pleaded with them not to go as someone else is going to get hurt but they went, and we never heard anything else. They were closed books and loyal to each other. That was the second time that happened, but we never found out anything, we prayed for all of them and we respected their privacy on some matters.

A few months after, we had been in the hall with the youth club, and the very two men from the council had been sitting in the car park. Each time a scooter or car parked up they asked the boys or girls, "Why do you come to this club called Gillingham Christian Youth Club?". Some of them told us about it, but we hadn't seen them. They were the ones who thought we would not last, two women. The council had confessed to us further down the line they didn't think we could do it. The same man came and presented us with a shield with Gillingham Christian Youth Club all shining on this special shield for all to see. Photos were taken, and we held the shield for a year as it was given to us because we were voted for doing the most for the community. It changed hands each year, but we held onto it proudly for all that time. God is so great; it was funny on the night we told the boys and girls that the men were coming to present it to us. We tried to keep everything tidy but when they walked through the door, one of the boys someone had put a picture up on the kitchen door of a nude woman. It was quickly taken down. It was a job keeping up with them, but it was fun as well. There was some music we wouldn't let them play in the club, and some of them tried each time to bring it in and play it. Through God everything was in control. He would let us know when we would say, "No, turn that one off".

We were introduced to someone who was very good to our club and a dear friend of Carole and me. He worked for I.T., which had a different meaning in those days. It stood for Intermediate Treatment. It meant we had to take some of the teenagers from the youth club, for it would be the last chance for them to attend before they were in deep trouble with the law. We did that, and he was a good help to the club. Sometimes he brought in money for equipment, and sometimes he would come in a van and say, "Come on, where are we going?" Then we go down to Margate, and the club loved it, and they liked him. He just got down and joined in with them. We had a snooker table, and lots of other equipment that he bought in. We did have a dartboard, but we had to put that away as they were throwing the darts at each other. He did take a video of the club one night but sadly that got lost along the way. Carole and I used to meet up on a Wednesday afternoon and pray. We asked the Lord, "What do you want to us to talk about that night?" We always waited on him, and he had told us what to say. We always said, "What would we do if he told us something different?", but he always told us the same thing in a quiet prayer time. He was in control.

CHAPTER 6

DROP IN

As well as running the Youth club in the summer holidays, we opened a drop-in club in the Salvation Army hall. The hall was in the middle of the town, and we had meetings with the youth leader. It started at the beginning of the summer break, and it was somewhere for the youth to come play games and talk etc. It was somewhere for the teenagers to go to in the daytime. It was good because many came in and once again they heard something about God. It was a busy time for us as we had also started up a club called the Friday Club in my old secondary school Upbury Manor. We had a meeting with the headmaster who was a Christian and each Friday, we held the club in the lunch break, talking about Jesus. At the first meeting, we had fourteen people turn up and ten of them gave their lives to Jesus. That was amazing! He always asked us if we needed anything for the youth club and we said we needed a blackboard. Straight away he gave us one which we used a lot in our discussions with the youth. In the 80s, it was all very exciting for Christians are there always seemed to be a good speaker in town, or a good Christian band, which we took the youth club to see many times.

We were going to a church in Gillingham called St. Marks. They had a lot of speakers and connections with the youth. One thing about the 80s was the lack of respect for women in the church, especially if you were on your own, like me.

I had joined the church's ladies group for a while but felt a little bit out of it. There was another girl who was on her own and we used to stay together. I was put in a home group that wasn't far from where I lived but sadly I felt like an outsider as they were all married couples. One day I had gone to the church on the Sunday morning and they were all speaking about how the meal was so good that they had eaten the night before. The meal had been held at the home group leader's house. I asked him why I wasn't included, and I was told, "We didn't think Ted would come so we didn't ask you". I would have liked to have been given the chance to invite Ted. That happened many times.

Ted was finding it difficult, as now the boys were coming to the meetings in church as well. Sadly, quite often on a Sunday morning we would have a row and I would walk to church crying inside the church. One week, it was so bad, that each time I began singing the chorus of God's love, I just cried quietly. One of the husbands of the ladies group had seen me crying, and after the service he came over to see what was wrong and why was I crying. We sat and talked in full view of all the church, but afterwards his wife had said, "Just because she hasn't got a Christian husband, she's not going to have ours." So once again, I'd come up against such bad feelings. It was bad enough going on my own, but it was also made worse by bad comments, so I left that church.

I moved on to a church in Chatham called "The Kings" church. We enjoyed it there. Eventually, I thought, yes, I want to become a member, so I made an appointment to see the pastor. In the office, I went in feeling so happy only to be told, "No, we cannot accept you as a member as you don't like men".

Can you imagine how I felt? Having a wonderful husband, three wonderful sons and their friends in and out of my home, I asked what made him think that and he said, "Because it's only you and another woman who run the youth club. You should have a man in charge". I explained that the youth club belonged to God first and men have come along with the idea of helping, but always change their minds when they see the club's boys and girls. It was not any other youth club with board games and making models, it was God's youth club. His youth club consisted of youngsters who had been banned from other youth clubs and out of prison. They came from all over, and yes, we were always open that if God wanted a man to help us we would pray about it. Many did look on, but never came back. Some of the youngsters did look threatening, but not to me and Carole. We had so much love for them and how much more did God love them.

We always had a party each year on our youth club birthday. One year, we thought we would have a fish and chip party. I remember going into the shop and saying to the man, "Can we have twenty-one portions of fish and chips please?" We always had a birthday cake, and we would have a party at Christmas with party hats and candles. We used to have so much fun. Eventually our time was at an end. We had to get out of the Hall. We searched and searched for somewhere but couldn't find anywhere. Our friend from IT took us all out a few times in the van, and we used the IT centre for a few weeks. We had a meeting with the Methodist minister in Gillingham, they had a fabulous hall over the church, and a coffee room was intertwined with it. It was great but when we asked about the cost it was about £20 each week, and we couldn't afford it. We only charged thirty pence to get in each week, and so many tried to get out of paying that, so we told her it was out of our reach.

To our joy, she said, "Oh, you can have it for five pounds". Thank you, Jesus, once again! He is in everything we do, we always prayed first, and God always provided. We had to go down a little dark alley to get to the hall, but the Youth club members loved it. There was a big main hall where they could play ball games as rough as they wanted to, and in the other room, it was just like a coffee bar.

We were so pleased with it. Some of the boys were nineteen and over and mostly scooterists, but not all of them were, they were very protective to me and Carole. One week in particular, there was a boy who was always trouble, especially when we asked him for his 30p. That week, he was a bit abusive and I said we can't keep letting him in without paying the admission as it was not fair on the others. One of the older boys heard this and said to me, "Is it causing you trouble Gail?" I said, "No, don't worry about it." Suddenly, he went missing and I never took any notice, he then turned up about five minutes later and said, "Here is the thirty pence, and he won't be abusive to you again." I said, "I hope you haven't hurt him", but they were so protective to us.

A lot of the club had been, and still were, involved in ghost hunting and the Ouija board. They knew about my past, but they still carried on with it. One night, some of them came back in the hall as we were closing, very scared as they had seen something when they were doing it. We had many discussions about it. We used to say, "What do you want to talk about tonight?", and of course they mostly wanted to talk about sex, we always discussed anything they wanted to talk about, but it always had to finish on God's view and how He saw it. Carole and I were shockproof so whatever they said we listened. At that time, it was the entire scare about Aids and HIV, so that was a very big topic. Nobody really understood much about it then, but there were always different views and fears about catching it from shaking hands or kissing. It was a very big question mark.

We had a big poster that some of the boys made that looked like a red brick wall. It was there for them to write on, or when we had visitors or bands to speak to them, we always asked them to write on it. I still have that poster; it is so precious with so many memories. Of course, some things we had to draw over as they were unacceptable, but we checked it each week. We had our own football team, and we even had our own kit which was given to us by my cousin. It was red and black, so we started arranging football matches against other churches and youth clubs. Our team always looked like the scariest rough and ready guys against the other teams, I felt sorry for some of their teams. I think they were afraid to tackle our players in the match. We went along to every game. Ted used to take them out training up on the field near where I grew up. He was the only other male they would listen to and he did a very good job of keeping them together as a team. They learnt a lot from him, and they enjoyed learning football skills as he was a good football player.

CHAPTER 7

DIFFERENT RULES

Many churches in the 80s enforced strange rules. At one of the churches, we took some of the boys from the youth club. They all arrived and sat down wearing their parkas complete with scooter badges, and their crash helmets under the seats, all well behaved. Then the pastor said, "When you become a Christian, you must change the way you look and dress." Well, that was another one that bites the dust! What were they thinking, what was wrong with these churches, and how did they expect ordinary people to come in and feel welcome?

There was one church that was good for them and talked to them. It was Parkwood Christian Fellowship. We all turned up one week with the boys and girls, and although some people looked at them strangely, most of them made them feel loved. We had seven of them who have given their lives to Jesus at that time, and wanted to be baptised, so it was arranged on a Sunday evening, we would have the baptisms. How proud we were to see this happen, they were fully immersed, and all given a word of scripture, each time they came up from the water. I have so many memories of that night; they all looked so good and so different to when we first met them. I have the video that was taken that night, it may be a bit scratchy now, but it is a wonderful memory of those precious days. We had a very special evening! Later, we all ended up at my house for tea and coffee. This happened quite a few times back at mine after church. Outside, about 12 scooters were parked up all the way up the road, bliss for us, but perhaps not so for our neighbours.

Later, that year, we had another four baptised at the same church. Carole and I had been visiting prisoners on a Sunday morning; we joined in their services at the church prison. Some of them were not allowed to come to the service as they were the ones that were classed as dangerous. After the service they would make us tea and we talk to them, they needed the love of Jesus just as much as anyone else. One of the prisoners was so upset as he had just found out his wife had left him for another man and there was not anything he could do. Another one of the prisoners had written on a large manuscript, a beautiful poem called, "The Four calls" for our youth club. This is the poem,

THE FOUR CALLS

The Spirit came in childhood and pleaded, "Let me in"
But oh, the door was bolted, by thoughtlessness and sin;
"I am too young," the child replied, "I will not yield today"
There's time enough tomorrow;
The Spirit went away.
Again, He came and pleaded
In youth's bright happy hour;
He came but heard no answer,
For lured by Satan's power
The youth lay dreaming then,
And saying, "Not today."
"Not till I've tried Earths pleasures".
The Spirit went away.
Again, he called in mercy
In manhood's vigorous prime
But still he found no welcome,
The merchant had no time.
No time for true repentance,
No time to think or pray,
And so repulsed and saddened
The Spirit went away.
Once more he called and waited,

The man was old and ill,
And scarcely heard the whisper,
His heart was cold and still.
Go leave me; when I need thee
I'll call for thee, he cried
Then sinking on his pillow,
Without a hope he died.

It was so special to us that he would do that for us, it meant a lot to our club. I still have the card he wrote it on, I treasure it. We had it hanging up in the club, it got a bit dirty as sometimes some of them took it down and it got tea stains on it, but it is still special.

CHAPTER 8

ANSWERED PRAYERS

So many people took a lot of interest in our youth club, and what was going on, but no one wanted to sponsor us at all. Carole and I walked the length of our high street one day trying to get some sort of sponsorship, which we needed for the football kit. No one wanted to fund us at all. Jesus always got us what we wanted and needed, and my cousin had given us a football kit that he had used before so here we go, all set for those games to be played. Red and black and they all look so smart in it. A wonderful lady we worked with arranged an evening in her home to raise money for our youth club. She was very special, and she had photos all around the room, and allowed us to talk about the club. She had visited the Youth club, and I think she realised how important it was to us both. We would arrange trips for the club. One weekend, we had all gone down to Margate with them all, it was a beautiful day and lots of fun. Another weekend, we had arranged to have a day at Sheerness with water sports arranged, and then we we're going to have a barbecue. Off we went with all the food in the car, but it didn't stop raining and it was so cold that we ended up in a café with all of them. I must admit, the owner looked a bit worried when he saw how many were coming in, but they were good, and we ended up back at my house for the barbecue, which had to be an indoor one, because all the food defrosted. Ted was amazing, he helped cook it all and the whole of my twenty-foot lounge was covered in boys and girls in soaking wet clothes because they had driven their scooters. It was a good and fun day anyway.

Another time, we were taking about ten of them to see a Christian band in Lordswood. We came out of the foyer at the end, and the young girl came running in the front entrance and said, "There is a gang of boys waiting outside to jump the boys when they leave". Why was it that everyone wanted to fight our youth club? As each person went out the door to go home, we could see this gang waiting outside, lots of them all looking angry and mean. Their faces were there each time the door swung open. We said, "Right come on, we have to pray, so we all stood round in the Foyer and prayed that they would go away and not return." Our wonderful Father is amazing and what a wonderful God we serve. After we had prayed with everyone else just walking past us and not taken any notice. We carried on praying and the doors swung open, and no one was there, no gang, no boys waiting for us at all. If I hadn't seen them myself, I probably would have thought perhaps they weren't there to start with, but they were, with all the mean and nasty looks they had of pure hate. Our Jesus sorted it out and they were no more to be seen. Another answered prayer.

Many times, we had prayers answered, and they knew that even though some of them didn't want to admit it. One night one of the boys came to the club high on drugs and troublesome. After a lot of aggro, we said he had to leave as we had to think of everyone else. Eventually, he left, as we had to drag him out of the toilet. He was so high and abusive, but without us knowing, he had gone outside and damaged some of their scooters that were parked in the car park, and one of the boys had said that he was trying to get in downstairs in our other exit door with another friend, who was also high.

Carole and I rushed downstairs to see if the door was locked. It had a bar across the middle which I was hanging onto tightly. I was trying to stop them coming in, and there was something being sprayed through the crack in the large door which was going down my throat. I couldn't let go as I was keeping the youth club safe. They didn't know what was going on at that time, if they did they would have sorted it for us, but we were thinking of them and their safety. They were angry when they found out what the two boys had done, and more so, when they saw how my breathing was affected. They had given up trying to light the petrol, about the same time I had let go of the door. My breathing was getting worse and I had to let go at the same time they must have moved away from the door. We found out afterwards that the spray was lighter fuel; they were trying to set the youth club alight. We found a whole box of matches, and the empty can at the door outside. Thankfully, once again, our Father God did not allow any matches to light, as if it had, it would have been so dangerous. I was on the other side of the door not knowing this, with lighter fuel down my throat. I had problems with my breathing all the way home that night, and for a long time afterwards I had to have a toxicology report done. I never let Ted know how bad I was at the time as I was worried he would want me to give it up, but when I had the report back, it said my breathing would be affected for the rest of my life. However, they did not have the best doctor, the one that I have, my God, would not let me be harmed. I often wondered what they would have thought afterwards when they come down from the fix. We never saw them again in the club; they were good boys but changed so much when they were high. Sadly, that was the story in those days.

There was a lot of glue sniffing back then. It was very strong as some of them used to put it on their scarves, so they could smell it all the time, but then so could everyone else. It used to make me feel sick sometimes as it was so strong. Some of the boys had made a large poster that looked like a red brick wall. They were all allowed to write things on this poster and when we had guests or live bands visiting, we asked them to sign it. I still have that poster; it was six years of good memories. At the end of each week we had to check it as some things were slightly unacceptable.

We had speakers and bands in those days, and some came to the club. It was usually just Carole and I speaking. I think over the years, they felt safe with us, we had a bond with them and some of them started to open about things. They would not have said in the beginning. We had an outreach for three weeks with Eric Delve speaking every night. We had attended so many meetings beforehand with youth leaders and churches that were involved in the outreach. It was a wonderful time. A lot of youth clubs turned up, as Eric Delve had a wonderful rapport with the youth. Carole and I were counsellors at the meetings, and some of the youth club came along. It was in a big tent on the Black Lion fields called 'Down to Earth'. It was a wonderful three weeks. Eric Delve was a very good speaker, and lots of people came forward to give their lives to Jesus. It was sad when it was over. I had asked Ted to come with us, but he made a lot of excuses. However, the day after it was over, we were sitting having a Sunday dinner and

Ted came out with something that Eric Delve had spoken about on the previous night. He had come along and sat in the back of the tent and none of us knew!

We trusted that whoever came to the youth club, God wanted there. We had a lot of fun times with them, especially when we all went out. When they went on their scooter runs, which was quite a few times, some of them would meet up and go from my home. I always enjoyed seeing the scooters parked outside my house. Many times, they would be parked up outside, and they would have some running problems with them. Ted would always be there to help, either to work outside, or take it round the back to the garden, through a narrow alley, and he would fix their scooters. He was good to them and he loved them also. In those days, we always had teenagers in the house as well, as our own boys, and their friends would be coming and going. We started a Bible study, one night a week, with anyone from the youth club who wanted to come. Sometimes, we would end up with someone just trying to prove God didn't exist, but they always went away with a lot of good teaching. Sometimes, I would have somebody who had been brought round through the lunch break, having a problem and wanted to talk, there were so many problems in the youth, and they just needed somebody to talk to. Some had bad problems and all we could do is pray for them.

CHAPTER 9

GOD'S PROTECTION

Around that time, I had written to Cliff Richard about the Youth club, and he sent us a photo, signed 'To Gillingham Cristian Youth club, from Cliff'. Following that, Carole and I were invited to his book launch in London. That was exciting for us. We were part of a group of people who just sat round and asked him questions. We felt very blessed that day.

In the time of 1987, when the big storm hit England, we had it bad in Kent. The night after the storm, we were taking the Youth club to see Nicky Cruz in a van driven by Ted. There were lots of trees and debris on the roads, so we were a bit late. We parked up where we could and managed to be seated just in time. When we came out, we found our van was blocked in, so the boys bumped the van out of the car park. To our shock, we realised we had parked in a police station. It was a good job they did not have CCTV then.

One week, one boy came in who did not come very often. He offered to make me and Carole a drink. We thought how nice of him. When he went off to the kitchen God said to me, "Don't drink the drinks, as he has put bleach in them." When he brought them out, we questioned him about it. He eventually admitted to it, but he was more interested in who had told us. When we told him, he did not believe us. Our Father was always protecting us. He was there through everything. He made the way before we even got there but it was always His Youth club and we were so blessed to be able to run it for Him. He never let us down. At the point when I will go home to be with Jesus, I pray I will see many faces of the people that came through the club, even if it was only one time they came. It was important they heard the Word and it will not leave them.

My sons are still close friends with a lot of the youngsters from the Youth club, and still see some of them. Many of them are married with families, but God's word never goes out void it will always stay with them and they will remember it when they least expect to. I do still pray for them. I met one of them two years ago, my son had arranged for him to meet me as a surprise. I was so happy to see him, and I just had this big hug from him, and he said to me, "I never forget all the things you taught us in the club". That meant so much to me, it made me so happy but also tearful at the same time.

CHAPTER 10

FREEDOM FROM THE DEMONS

We were having great teaching from a couple from Rainham Parkwood church, the meetings were held in their home. It was there that I had deliverance ministry for all the things I was into in my past. The enemy was still trying to keep control. I had two very strong Christian men pray over me. The hold was gone. It took a while, but I came home free from any demons that were still trying to hang on. Praise God I was clean, and I was sure I was going to stay that way. My Father gave a scripture that night;

"Believe on the Lord Jesus Christ and your whole entire household shall be saved."
(Acts Chapter 16:31-32)

I took that on board, and I stand on that promise every day. We had special evenings learning all of Derek Prince studies on blessings and curses. Also, we learnt about soulish ties, soulish talk and self-imposed curses etc. It was the best teaching that I had heard. Even to this day, I have had a lot of teaching but the best in all my thirty-nine years of trusting God, Derek Prince was the best teacher. If I could only choose one, it would be him; it has stayed with me throughout, and has made me wary of what I buy or receive, or what not to bring into my home. About that time, I had a real thorough clear out in my home and found so many inappropriate books, so I burned them. I did not want anything that was going to hinder my walk with God or bring a curse into my house or family.

Thankfully, even now to this day, God still gives me that discernment. If I look at things to buy, I know what is okay and what not to have. I had a necklace that was given to me when I was a little girl. It was black and I realised that it had scarab beetles all the way around it. That had to go, so I took it outside and smashed it up with a hammer. It took a while to break up and walking across the middle of it, as if it had come out of the necklace, was a live scarab beetle. Very spooky, but it is the truth the enemy will use anything to have a hold on you, so make sure that he cannot, by checking what is in your home. Do not underestimate what he can sneak in as he wants that hold on you. You must make sure you don't make it easy for him. Derek Prince speaks of many things that change in a Christian home when you have got rid of objects or books. Peace has come. You must remember to pray as well, against any hold that the object may have had on you or your home. He was a humble man but when it came to God's word, he was on fire to teach the truth. Even some record covers that I see in the shops, or signs with the 'all-seeing eye' on the magazines, I would not have in my home. I have so many people say to me, "It's not harmful; it's just a bit of fun." Especially around Halloween, why do people want their children to go around dressed as a demon, or the devil? I do not understand why some children know more about Halloween then they do about Christmas or Easter. I don't understand why some parents let their children have books about casting spells. It is another ploy for the enemy to get the children interested and another reason for the parents to say, "It's just a bit of fun."

The same applies for tee shirts. How much the enemy is creeping in without a lot of people realising it. The enemy is very subtle; he can creep in so quietly into so many things. You must be on guard all of the time. Think before you buy, there is so much out there these days, even more so because people don't think first. Don't have anything that gives glory to the enemy. Some of the Youth club used to bring things in that they thought could be wrong or holding a curse on them. They would ask Carole and I to get rid of them. We used to go opposite the club to a main drain in the road and put the items down it. We would all stand around and pray against any hold or curse that would be entangled with them. I often wondered what the neighbours thought we were doing on those nights, but it was always the choice of the youth club member. We made that clear to them.

CHAPTER 11

NEW JOB

In those days, we saw arms growing out with prayer and there was a man who had an accident, and his foot was mangled up. We all prayed for him and his foot healed, perfectly in front of us. I always looked forward to those meetings. In 1985, a friend from the IT centre had come to see me and called to say there were two job positions going for Residential Social Workers, working with teenagers. He said he had put a 'good' word in for us, telling the boss how well we worked with the youth. We went to be interviewed and we both got the job straight away. I loved that job it was obviously different to the Youth club. We were restricted to rules this time, so we couldn't speak to the children about God unless they asked us to.

One girl asked me to tell her about Jesus, as her Grandad was a Christian, so that was a very good morning at work. Another time, while I was at work on a Sunday morning, one of our girls wanted to go to church, so we took her to ours where she had prayer. My friend told me after a while, when they knew two Christian women were starting work there, they thought we would turn up with thick stockings and buns in our hair. Isn't the perception strange the way people look at how they see Christians? We were both very different to that, and some of the staff asked us about our faith. We had to sleep in one or two nights a week so there was plenty of time to chat once the kids are all gone to bed.

At that time, my boss used to talk about the Women's Refuge. The lady who ran the home was a Christian, so I took some things to them for the Children. I kept going back as I had a heart for them. The following Christmas, I asked the lady in charge how many girls, and how many boys were going to be there for Christmas.

I did not want to know their names, but roughly how old they were. I went out with Ted, with the list and bought a present for each one. There were about thirty-six children there at that time. I enjoyed doing that so much and some of the teenage girls that were coming into my home at that time came one Sunday afternoon and helped me wrap them all up. I carried that on as I had joy from that. I found out that the postmen from our town at that time gave them a Christmas party, and a really good time was had by all. I thought what a wonderful thing for them to do. My son and I dropped the gifts off in big bags and it was so exciting to be able to do that. I kept in touch with them until I left my job. When I first moved to Cornwall, I was able to get in touch with someone who helped at a refuge so once again I was able to send in some children's clothes as they often turn up in the middle of the night with nothing.

In my job working with the children in care, it was not always easy. There were a few times that my life was in danger, but my Father kept me safe. I had been threatened with knives and some wanted to gouge my eyes out with a fork and lots more. Sometimes, I think now, "Why did I do it?", but I did, and it's all in the past now. The place where I worked was a family centre at first, but then it changed to an adolescent centre, and the whole atmosphere changed, as we had a lot of dealings with the police. Once again, there was a lot of interest in the occult, and a lot of the Children had been deeply involved. My boss used to ask us what things meant or what does astral travelling mean. He was good, as he knew Carole and I ran the Youth club on a Wednesday so he knew we could not work on that day.

There was a lot of times when it became really dangerous working there, especially as in those days there were only two people on shift in the evening, One of them used to have to take some of the kids out to see their parents, so it left only one person in the home alone with the rest of the residents. The police station was along the road to us and we would receive a phone call saying, "We have one of your boys or girls here, they've just broken up the police cell, and we are just going to bring them home to you." You got ready for a rough time, I cannot say anything about the cases we had there, but once again God used us to a very high limit. He also protected us so much in so many areas of our work there, so many times we were in a very sticky situations and God saw us through.

When Carole and I worked together on an evening shift, once all the kids were sorted in bed and asleep, we would sit and have a coffee and a prayer. We were always thankful that we could work together. One of the girls in the house went to the local spiritualist church one week. She knew my dad went there, and when she came home that night she looked upset and I carried on getting her supper she said, "Gail, I spoke to your dad and I said to him, I know your daughter." He replied, "I haven't got a daughter". She was so upset for me, but I was used to it. She was very close to me after that as I feel she felt sadness for me from that day on, but she knew that I understood about rejection.

CHAPTER 12

BROKEN PROMISES

During that time working in the home, Darren had gone up to see my Dad. He had taken some photos with him that had been taken over the last few years. I did not let him take any of me or Ted, just the boys. Dad had asked if he could keep them to show my Mum as she was out. We never got them back and when both of my parents had died, I asked my Auntie if she could retrieve the photos for me. She said that my Dad had taken them up the garden and put them on a bonfire. It was hard for me to believe that. Did they hate me that much? In my job in the Adolescent Centre, my boss was very good to me. He had realised I had a problem with my past, so he counselled me once a week for an hour before my shift. He pointed out a lot of things for me about my past that helped me. When I was very young, my mum used to say that I would end up in a children's home, my boss said, "Yes Gail, you did, but you are working and helping the children". Words spoken!

Parents, watch what you say to your children, and only speak good and loving words to them. Tell them how much you care for them, and how important they are to you. Tell them how much you love them. Remember, your words stay with your children, they do not forget what their parents speak over them or to them. Do not speak curses over them with negative words, not even in a joke. Think that each word you speak is very important, and make sure you speak blessings over them. Your words will follow them through their lives and though their families lives too. Make every moment count! I made sure I would never treat my sons badly. I love them with an unconditional love, and I want them to know how proud I am of them. I will never forsake them or leave them. I respect them and they will make choices through their lives and I pray for them always. It was my choice to become a Christian and it was sad that my family thought I was wrong. I chose to become a Christian, but I lost my family because of that choice, but it should not have been like that, as I was still me.

One Father's day, after this had happened I was upset, and my Jesus gave me the scripture;

"When my father and mother forsake me, the Lord will take care of me" **(Psalm 27:10)**

What precious love He has for us Abba Father that's who He is to me. It was nearly nine years that I worked in the adolescent centre. I loved it at first as it was a family centre. We would start our shift at two o clock in the afternoon until nine thirty the next morning. We had some fun in the beginning. We took the children out and spent a lot of time with them. Later, when it changed to an adolescent centre, so much changed, it became a different place. Something happened to me there that left a very bad mark on my life, and in 1993 I knew I had to leave. I knew at that moment that I would never go back there again.

It was a very bad time for me, personally. I had lost so many people at that time, some had died, some had just gone out of my life and one of my best friends, my dog Jessie had died too. It was a very painful time for me, and I could not cope. I had lost six people who had died that were very close to me, so very quickly my life had taken a downfall, and I felt I was slowly shutting down. That is where the agoraphobia and social agoraphobia set in, and I was too weak to stop it. I shut myself away from the world. My parents and my family had disowned me for being a Christian, and my three sons had moved to Cornwall. Alone and feeling suicidal, poor Ted once again had to deal with his desperate wife who felt everyone, and everything had let me down. People who were supposed to be friends were not around. You find out who your true friends really are when you are down and out. Alone and feeling suicidal, and everyone abandoning me, I cried out to God, "I thought you had forgotten me, why me Lord?" I felt abandoned and left alone, the hurt was more than I could bear. Where were the people that had promised to be there for me? Why was this allowed? I was in no way ready to try to understand. I just wanted to get out. I had put a wall up before me to keep me safe, there were only a few people in my life that I had allowed to break it down, but as soon as someone hurt me, that wall went straight up again. Even now I am still a builder of that defence wall.

For over five years, I was shut in my own home. I was so depressed, and I used to try and think how I could kill myself without it being suicide. I couldn't laugh or even smile, I just wanted it to finish. Ted left for work at 7:30 in the morning and I never saw or heard from anyone until he comes home at tea time. I had to cling on to my faith even though I did not have all the answers. I had one good friend, Audrey, who came to see me through the time I was shut indoors. She would sometimes take me out for a coffee. I could go with her as I could only go if I could trust the person to bring me back. It sounds silly now, but when you have agoraphobia it makes you feel very weak in people's company. It is important to feel you have their trust. Someone had said to me that they wanted to drive me somewhere local and leave me there to make my way back. They thought that would be a cure, but it would have been the opposite for me. Audrey was a very good friend of mine, someone who I had worked with at the adolescent centre. We had worked our twenty-four hour shifts together, so we knew each other very well, you had to, as in that job, you had to be in tune with each other and one step ahead of the kids in the home. We had some fun with some of the kids, but also some rough times. She would phone me and tell me she was coming, so I would look out for her and open the door. It all sounds sad now, but that was the way I was then, and I needed good friends around. Sadly, there was not that many who was there at that time. A few came to see me from work once with a card and present, but I never saw them again after that. At that time, I also had to go through my mum's and Dad's funeral feeling so sad that my brothers did not want me there. They even passed my window as my brothers lived close by, so it was painful for me. Rejected, and upset at losing them I could not mourn with the rest of my family. I cried so much to God, "How much more Lord?" The worst thing was that no one came from church to see me and that made Ted very angry, as he was upset for me, and it was not a very good witness to him at all. The silence went on and on and the hurt did not want to go away.

CHAPTER 13

NEW BEGINNINGS

In the summer of 1995, Ted bought me Sky TV to watch the film channels, and once again God was in this, as the God channel had just started a few hours a day. I would set my video and watch it during the next day. At first, I could not stand the fact that everyone was so happy, and I was having pity parties myself. I learnt a hard lesson from Joyce Meyer. She had told the story of her life, and then she looked straight at the camera and said, "Stop having those pity parties and get back up!"

It was as if she was talking to me. I jumped up and turned the TV off thinking, "Who does she think she is, she doesn't know my life", but then I quickly put the TV back on again and listened. "Don't let your past invade your future", that was so true that it made me realise that day, what I was allowing the enemy to do. I had allowed him to pull me down and not get back up again. It really spoke to me.

That was the start of learning all I could from those few hours a day. I watched every moment and learnt about standing on the Word. I set out my prayers and wrote them on paper and stuck them on my fridge door. I prayed that I would have a bungalow in Cornwall with a beautiful garden with birds singing. I cut out a picture from the Cornish paper of a bungalow just like the one I envisaged that I would have. The bungalow that God gave me a few years later was the replica of the one on my prayer list, Praise God! He goes to every detail! I stood on the Word and trusted Him. I studied Charles Capps teaching and I was fervent on my prayers. There were set backs and down times. We had rented a bungalow where the boys stayed, and Ted and I came down at weekends when the boys lived there. My life was so different when I was in Cornwall, but I was sad when I had to go back. We had looked at a bungalow, but we realised we did not have enough for the deposit as we had not sold ours yet. I had to go and phone the estate agent and tell him we must let it go. I cried all the way back to the rented place which we had to vacate as the owners needed it back. My life was so broken; I had held on to that dream and it was smashed in one day. Ted and I had to pack up and return to Kent. The boys managed to rent another bungalow, but I sobbed all the way home. It was as if I was going back to prison, as I knew I would have to be in prison once again in my own home. I felt so lonely and broken. I remember the next morning, just looking at all the boxes we had brought back from Cornwall, and once again, the tears flowed. I felt defeated.

Back to my prayers, it was very hard to get back up again. I had to pick myself up and go on. I could have easily just caved in and given in, but, "No Gail, Stand and keep standing!" Stand even when you feel you cannot stand anymore. I stood until I ached inside with confusion. I did not know what was going on inside of me or what was going on around me. I was afraid of what I could see in the natural, but I had to see what was going in the Supernatural, so I just had to keep going on with my prayers. Stand, and stand again.

At Christmas 1998, we rented a bungalow to spend our Christmas in Newquay. We had become Grandparents in the previous October to our first wonderful grandchild, Lee's firstborn, Lewis. We packed up all our decorations and food and set off. It was so enjoyable once again, but we had to return to Kent, but it was even harder now as we had to leave our grandson as well. We used to come down every other two weeks to see them; there wasn't Facetime then, so we saw a change in Lewis each time we arrived. I was still having problems at home, still not going out and still not seeing anyone. This went on for over five years, and I had to do something about it. I became very brave and told Ted I was getting in touch with the man we rented the place off over Christmas and ask him if I could stay there until Easter, when he starts the holiday rentals again.

My Father was in on it as he said yes, and he let me have it for a decent price. I don't think Ted thought I would go on my own, but I had to, as I was still being tormented with the memories at home. I packed up some boxes and off I went. It was very hard to keep saying goodbye to Ted each time he came down, but I knew in my heart I had to do it to save myself. I found a church near where I was staying which was called Rhema Life. It was run by a couple from the American base in Newquay. I felt so at home there and loved that I could walk along the beach and spend time with Lee and his family. Ted and I had been looking at homes for sale and we went to see some. There wasn't the good feeling on most of them, or they were too much money. Ted had come down that Easter and we looked through the book in the estate agents. I was ready to get a rented flat, but Ted said, "No, we will look at this one". When I looked at it, I thought it was too much money. It was a lot more than we had been looking at spending, but Ted was adamant, so we went and looked at it. All I can say is that as we drove along a short private lane to three bungalows, ours was in the middle. I fell in love with it before I had even seen inside. We went around the back to a beautiful, large garden full of all sorts of lovely birds and I knew this was the one my Father wanted for me. Ted loved it too, so straight away we put the balls in motion. A week later, the owners put the price up as someone had offered more money. Once again, my Jesus allowed me and Ted to put that extra money together in the natural, I would say, "How? But God isn't in the natural. He is in the Supernatural, so it was ours. We moved in our home in July. I was on cloud nine and the bungalow was so much the same as I still have the prayer sheet for the bungalow.

CHAPTER 14

PRAYERS AND PROMISES

I still have that prayer bungalow today, as a reminder of what God will do for us if we trust in Him. I remember my Pastor coming around to see me. He walked round the garden, took an apple off the tree and said, "Gail, do you realise God has given you everything that you had on your prayer list, even down to the birds singing in the garden?" My Father is so precious! Some people give up too easily. They pray in faith, but after a while they give up not knowing that their prayers and their breakthrough could have been just around the corner. They give up too soon. I am a fighter, especially in prayers, I have Jesus in my corner, and I will make it with Him. I did not have anyone else praying for me, or with me. No church, no Christian friends, just me and Jesus. Who else would I need? If you are being tested, PASS THE TEST! It's an open book test; you have the author living inside of you. He said, "I will bring all things to your remembrance", and then He says, "I will make a way out of it. When that thing becomes so rough, I am going to send My anointing, and while you are standing, that anointing will remove the burden and destroy the yoke. Then the glory will be revealed inside of you. When My anointing shows up you will see the manifested Glory right before your eyes, so keep standing, until your answers come, and they will come, do not give up."

"Is My Word like a fire? Says the Lord, and like a hammer that breaks the rock in pieces?" **(Jeremiah 23:29)**

"Call upon those things that be not as though they were." **(Romans 4:17)**

My Father gave me these words in my prayer time:

My daughter, I will bless you with all that I have, I will allow you to have all that your heart desires, and more to give to others. You will be a blessing to many never fear about your future and do not allow negative words or thoughts to enter in. I am your provider your Abba Father see what I am in your eyes. I love you Gail, you have stood strong and firm through so many adversaries. You have been knocked from side to side, yet you still go on, and I know you will reap from your loyalty and faithfulness. Where others failed and returned to their old life, you stand firm with Me. Once again still standing strong and secure in Me. Amen to that my Jesus. Confession of faith has set me free, I just made sure I confessed each day over and over what God has promised to His children in His Word. His promises are Yes and Amen. Gods promise to bless by oath, this hope we have as an anchor of the soul, both sure and steadfast. I am an heir, I have inherited the promise, that in blessing God will bless me, rebuke you unbelief, I have Jesus, I have the word of God. I have the power of the Holy Spirit and His anointing. I am a covenant child of God, He does not lie. These scriptures are from Hebrews 6 and like Moses I patiently endured and I received my promise.

Many people wanted to know how I prayed for my home and how they could receive the same blessings. We had a mortgage on the bungalow; it was for twenty-five thousand pounds. This was more money than our home in Kent, so once again, my praying and standing stood firmly as Ted did not want a mortgage when he retired. Pray without ceasing and in 2004, our bungalow was paid for, debt free. God allowed the money to come in. Thank you, Jesus! I stood and prayed, and I patiently endured, then I received the promise, my bungalow was mine. It was my promise from God. I receive it in Jesus's Name, it was mine, paid in full. Amen and Amen. I speak these words into existence, and I prophecy over them. They have come to pass already. I see the manifestation of His word. I frame my world by the words spoken through my mouth. I based those declarations on the Word of God.

"My Father said, you shall have what you speak, you will have what you ask for, you will have what you say. Are you going to stay with the one who says you cannot or the Word that says you can! If you need healing, then pray the healing scriptures and promises. Claim them to come to pass, if you need wisdom ask for

wisdom, I ask for the wisdom of Solomon ask, and it shall be given unto you. Ask for protection to your family your church and pray for wisdom for your government, pray without ceasing. You can pray wherever you are. You do not have to be sitting comfortably or in a church building, just pray whether you are walking or just admiring the view somewhere. Thank Him for all that He has done and is still doing for you and what He will do for you in the days to come. I think that is something that a lot of Christians forget to do. God answers so many prayers and so many times Christians forget to praise Him for what He has done. I still walk around my garden and thank my Jesus for what He has blessed me with, I will never take for granted His amazing love for me and my love for Him." **(Mark 11:23-24)**

I was still enjoying going to the Rhema Life church, but because most of the people that went were mainly from the American base, after a few years they all had to return home to America as the base was closing. That was very sad, as each week it seemed we were having to have a farewell party and I hate goodbyes. When they had all gone, I didn't go to a church for a while; it was always going to be difficult as I don't drive so I used to watch Revelation TV. On Sunday mornings, they have a service that is called 'Church without walls'. I took bread and wine with them and I enjoyed the service. I was still studying the Word, praying hard and claiming my promises. I had special times with my Jesus, but I did crave sometimes the fellowship with people who loved Him as I do. I had prayed for Ted's salvation for so long I used to worry about him as he would not converse about anything to do with God. He said it was my thing although he would always pray with me when any of our family was travelling, or anyone felt ill, we would pray but he would just say Amen and agree with me. I continued to pray for him and all my family.

I had spent all my Christian life on my own. It is a lonely time of not having anyone to share your love of Jesus with people who have wives or husbands who share the love of God with each other. If you have some people in your church who are on their own, be a bit thoughtful towards those people that do not get to talk about Jesus all week, only at church on a Sunday. Try to put yourself in their position and think about what it is like once you leave the church building. Some may not get to talk about their needs or their joys until the following week. Think about them and talk to them. Sometimes I would come home from a meeting and feel so happy, but when you don't have anyone who wants to hear about it, you feel sad. That is why when some people have asked me what I think about someone who wants to marry someone who does not feel the same way as you; I have said I would not do it, as you cannot be unequally yoked. It does not work. As much as Ted and I loved each other, he could not understand the way I felt, and I could not understand what he found so difficult in me being different. I was not a Christian when Ted and I married. I thought I was, and so did Ted. However, you are different when one of you becomes born again, you are on different wave lengths, but then God knew how it would end, Praise His Name!

CHAPTER 15

TED'S SALVATION

Ted was seventy in 2016, and we all went to Lanzarote for a holiday to celebrate in October. He really enjoyed it and so did we. When we came back from the holiday, Ted had to have some blood tests carried out, and there were a few question marks. I made him go to the doctors, although he fought me, but I made the appointment. The tests were not good and Ted was taken into hospital. That was the start of many visits, and nights spent in Treliske Hospital. One night, he walked into our lounge and said, "I want to become a Christian". I remember saying, "What did you say?", and he repeated it. I remember saying okay and rushed around. I had waited and prayed for this moment for thirty-seven years. I had worried and prayed for him for so long, and now here he is asking the very thing that I had prayed for. What a joy and a relief that Ted had asked Jesus into his life. He told the nurses when he went into hospital that he was a Christian and he took in declarations of the Word of God in his pocket. I have a very special message on my phone from him. Each night I would ring Ted just before I went to sleep to see how he was. The message said, "Still praising the Lord".

None other than my close family could understand how much that message means to me. It was something that I waited for thirty-seven years to hear. Praise God! When he was in hospital, one of the boys said to him, "What made you become a Christian Dad, after all these years?". Ted replied, "Well I know your Mum has always prayed for me, and I watched this young chap on television that mum had taped, and what he said made sense". He had heard Rheinharde Bonnke, Jessie Duplantis, Amy Grant and Nicky Cruz, so many big names, but it was Daniel Chand that he listened to and I thank and praise God for him. He had been on Revelation television, and he had given his testimony of how God had saved him from his old life, and how God had worked in his new life with Him. Thankfully, that testimony had spoken to Ted. In March, Ted went home to be with his Lord and Saviour. I never got to share my life with Ted as a Christian husband for long, but I know he is home with Jesus, and when it is my time to go home, he will be there, and we will be together for ever. Praise God!

I contacted Daniel Chand and told him how God had used him to reach Ted. He sent me a lovely reply, and Daniel and Tanya, his wife, have become good friends of mine. They are very special to me and I love them very much. They pray for me if I need prayer, and they are so on fire for getting people to know Jesus. They are out there always doing what we all should be doing, getting people into the kingdom of God and that's what they do! Their ministry is called 'Walking like Jesus', and they are on fire for God. I also got in touch with Revelation TV, as they also reached Ted's heart as without them, Ted would not have heard the truth from someone else other than me.

I had found the end of my rainbow. I had a very special husband, three wonderful sons, and four special grandchildren; Lewis, Harvey, Ella and Joseph. They are very special to me and Ted was very proud of his grandchildren. They mean so much to him, and they do to me.

What a blessing children and grandchildren are to us, and we must pray they have a blessed life.

Here I am, now seventy years old, and I started a new transition in my life. I do more now than I have done for a long time. I love my church, Wave House in Newquay. I have very special friends there and the church does a lot for the community, young and old. Now, I help in a small group, we take Jesus to the Nursing Homes. We sing the old hymns with them, and we have a word and we always end with the prayer of salvation. I enjoy seeing them each week, and they say the prayer with us. I wonder how many we will see when we go home to Heaven. Doing God's work makes me happy, and the most treasured thing about it all is seeing someone come to know Jesus as their Saviour. Each time that brings joy and I never take that for granted. I am amazed at what God can do for me and for others. I could never be bored, as each day is a new beginning in the life of a

Christian, and I would not want to live any other way. I have in front of me, my Bible at the following scripture:

"To you oh Lord I will sing praises." **(Psalm 101:1)**

I will sing praises to my most high God. He has brought me out of such a dark place, to a place of unconditional love and happiness. A place of trust and rest and a place of security and perfection. What would I say? He is my Jesus, my Lord, He is my God!

He, above all had given me my pot of gold in all that I have, and I know that He alone has always been there for me even when I didn't know it. He was there from the beginning, but I didn't know it, and I came through stronger, still holding on to those promises that my Father had given me. Promises that I had prayed over my situations my family, my past my frustrations, and when things looked bleak. I would cry out to God, shout at Him sometimes, telling Him I was sorry, and I would get back up and stand on the Word of God once again. I would claim my promises over my life and people around me. Sometimes, I have said them through gritted teeth, especially when it looked bleak, but stand and stand again. Yes, sometimes it has been tough when things around do not look like they are ever going to change or work out, but that's where faith comes in. I never stopped believing that God would answer my prayers, through so many heartaches and pitfalls and reasons to give up. I continued to, "Stand and keep standing".

You cannot give up on speaking the Word of God over your situations. Your breakthrough could be just around the corner, but you could lose it because you have given up and given up on God. I stood for nearly three years for my promise of a bungalow in Cornwall. We didn't have enough money. The value of our home in Kent would not have been enough to buy the bungalow in Cornwall. However, even before I knew it, my Father had put into the seller's mind to put their home up for sale at the right time as they were going to let it out before selling it, but God had other plans, and everything fell into place in God's timing. I had stood for all that time on what God had promised me and I am so glad I didn't give up.

CHAPTER 16

THE WORD OF GOD

The Word of God is powerful, blessings or curses. It is what comes out of your mouth that defines you. You must watch your words that you speak. Don't tell God how big your problem is; tell your problem how big your God is. Watch what comes out of your mouth. You can speak blessings or curses. Death and life are in the power of the tongue. I had learnt from an early stage in my Christian life about blessings and curses, and I have said it before, I had learnt from the best Christian teacher of all, Derek Prince. I went through many tapes and videos of his teaching, he was the best. Also, I learnt from him about bringing in satanic objects or books into your home that can bring in a curse. Check your children's books, what people think are a bit of fun can be very dangerous to your family. I have had people think I go too far into what I will not accept in my home, but I will not compromise the Word of God. I will not turn a blind eye to rubbish from the enemy or to anything that promotes his work, as I said earlier; remember he is subtle, so always watch what comes in. In the early days of the eighties, I got rid of anything that I thought was from the enemy, especially jewellery.

*"Take the sword of the Spirit which is the Word of God, with Gods word it is a weapon to use in all things." **(Ephesians 6:17)***

"These words are power packed, death and life are in the power of the tongue." **(Proverbs 18:21)**

Therefore, we must be very careful about what we speak. If you go around speaking only what you cannot do, instead of what you can do you will have to reap the consequences. Angels are waiting for you, they are listening to what you speak, and once again they are sent to minister to you, they are a vital part of your life.

"Angels are ministering spirits sent forth to minister for those who will inherit salvation." **(Hebrews 1:14)**

Angels carry out God's plans; you have angels working for you, so be careful what you speak. If you only speak negative and depressing things over you and your life, then they are probably sitting there with their arms folded. If you speak God's word over your life and blessings and promises from the word of God, then they will go on that assignment for you. Many times, angels helped in the days of the youth club, and when I worked with the teenagers in care. Speak protection over your life and your family's lives; send those angels out with God's blessing to protect you and your family. We must put a guard over our mouths, and only speak what the word of God says, not what we say, or the pain in our bodies say, but what Gods word says.

I have a book of promises and prayers that God gave me in the nineties to speak from His word over my life, and my family's lives. I speak them and believe that they are coming to pass, even though one of them was given to me a long time ago. I still stand and will continue to stand on that promise, it is in the word and I stand on the Word, so I know it will come to pass!

"Bless the Lord you his angels who excel in strength, who do His word, heeding the voice of His word, bless the Lord all you His hosts." **(Psalm 103:20-21)**

How exciting is His word, in the life of a child of God? We are covenant children of God, and God doesn't break His covenant. If you feel down or discouraged, or even afraid, shout to the enemy. Speak the spoken word of God and learn Rhema words to speak over your situation. Christ has redeemed us from the curse of the law, I refuse death and curses, I choose life and blessings. Sit with your bible in front of you and ask the Holy Spirit to give you promises to write down. Scriptures that have power and meaning to your life and your circumstances and speak them every day. If you have healing scriptures, Derek Prince said to speak them each time you sit down to eat. If they were tablets you would take them three times a day so likewise speak God's healing scriptures the same way.

Check out any objects, books or anything that you think is not of God, burn it or throw it away. It could be a hindrance to your prayers not being answered. Do not give them away as you could be passing on a curse to someone else, get rid of anything that could be a hindrance to your relationship with God. Pray over your house and your family's homes, pray over every journey they take, cover the vehicle that they travel in. Walk through your home in every room praying in the Spirit. Plead the Blood of Jesus over everything. Pray over your children's beds and tell Satan he is not going to invade their lives with his lies. I especially plead the Blood over my family when they are travelling. The devil seeks out people, especially teenagers and young people who have low self-esteem, he tries to manipulate them. He gets into their minds, but if we speak blessings over our family, we reap blessings, but if we only speak negative words over them, we can bring on a curse. We can be so complacent that we think everything is going to be ok in our lives, but we must never forget we have the power of the Holy Spirit living inside of us. We have all that we need to pray, all the right things over our families.

"I can do all things through Christ who strengthens me." **(Philippians 4:13)**

Let us pray in earnest over our children, our grandchildren, we will not let the enemy have control! We have a solid foundation; stand against the fiery darts of the enemy. People must see Jesus in you. Every time you meet someone, do not condemn them; show God's love through you. We cannot set ourselves aside from anyone who we think is different to us, show God's love, and that is all we need to do. There is a battle going on, Satan wants your family not to be happy or succeed, he wants your children, your peace of mind and your time. Are you going to let him in and take control, or are you going to rise up and fight with everything that is inside of you? God has given you all the tools, His Word, His Love and the Blood of Jesus. What more could you need? Make sure you continue with all the fire inside of you to win your family back to Jesus, and even if they are strong with Him, you can still pray to keep them there. Stand and Keep Standing. How many times my Father had to remind me of that! In the past, I have put anointed oil on Ted's pillow and prayed over it, I had a prayer cloth in my Bible with a photo of Ted in it. I tried so many things, but the greatest and toughest way is to speak the Word of God over each member of your family. The Word of God does not return void. David was a shepherd boy. He did not fight the giant with just his sling and a rock; he killed him with the Word of God.

"You come to me with a sword, with a spear, and with a javelin, but I come to you in the name of the Lord of Hosts, the God of the armies of Israel whom you have defied. This day the Lord will deliver you into my hand and I will strike you and take your head from you. And this day I will give the carcasses of the camp of the philistines to the birds of the air and the wild beasts of the earth that they may know that there is a God in Israel. Then all this assembly shall know that the Lord does not save with sword and spear, for the battle is the Lords and He will give you into our hands." **(1 Samuel 17:45-47)**

He had confidence, not in his strength, but in his God's strength.

"Not by might nor by power but by My Spirit, says the Lord of Hosts." **(Zechariah 4:6)**

There is no road that is too long that God cannot walk with you. He is love everlasting, His promises are yes and Amen. He loves you. With all the uncertainty in this world and all what is going on around us, I don't know how anyone can be without God. No-one knows what tomorrow will bring, I am not ashamed of my faith in God I have been both sides of the fence and I know which one the best is. Your last breath on earth will be your first breath in heaven or hell, which one will you choose? I have trusted in so many things when I was growing up but there is only ONE who I can trust in, JESUS! He will never let me down. God has brought me a wholeness that only He can give, I belong to Him. I am His child, His daughter, and I know He will never let go of me. I will never leave you or forsake you, knowing my Jesus is with me always. How could I fail even in my darkest days, He was with me. He has brought me through many trials and tribulations and heartbreaks. Sometimes I just want to sit with Him, as I know He will not let me down as man does. As you invite the Lord into your situation, the storms will die down and peace will come, and you will be restored. It is time to rest in the promises of God, get up and rise above your situation. Invite God in and watch for a miracle.

CHAPTER 17

STILL STANDING

Ted was and still is the love of my life. The moment he became a child of God, I felt a lot of pressure taken away from me, even though I was broken inside because he was so ill. My Jesus knows what lies ahead for us, and although it was a very sad and painful time. When Ted went home to be with Jesus, knowing that he was home in heaven, helped me to get through those days. I can remember going back to the crematorium two days after with the boys, as they wanted to look at the flowers. I didn't get out of the car, as I could not look at them and read the messages. I was praying, and I said to God, "I suppose this is Ted's resting place now and he said so clearly, "Teds resting place is not there, he is with Me". Once again, His peace came over me. I know that when it is my time to go home, I know Ted will be waiting for me with his arms open wide, so it is just like he has gone to live somewhere else for a while. When I see him again, we will be together forever. No more separation, no sadness, and my Jesus will be there with us.

At the time of Ted going home, me and my boys had an angelic experience that no one can deny, and me and my sons will always treasure that moment in our hearts. We thank God for it, and He made it so clear that Ted was with Him, safe and secure in His love.

My life changed quite a bit having to get used to saying 'I' instead of 'we', or 'us'. I had spent fifty-four years identifying 'me' as 'us', so it takes a while to change. My sons and grandchildren helped me so much, we were all hurting but we stayed strong together. We laughed at some of the things Ted used to say, he was so loved by us all. We have wonderful memories that no one can take away, and he had put so much of himself into my sons. I see so much of Ted in them, and the grandchildren, I see part of Ted in all of them. The night before the funeral, we were going down to Watergate beach to watch the sunset. That was something that Ted loved to do, and we thought that would be a good thing for us to share. I remember on the way down, the sun became covered with the darkest of clouds, and it looked bleak, that there would not be a sunset tonight. Even I said, "Oh, I don't think we are going to see that tonight", and I remember Lee saying, "Where's your faith mum", and we carried on. We parked up and walked down to the beach and suddenly, the sun came out, and the most glorious sunset was there to be seen. We just enjoyed it and made the most of it taking photos. I am sure God gave us that moment, as we wanted that for Ted. I have such a precious family; they are there for me, as I am there for them.

This year, it was the two-year anniversary of Ted going home. I had phone calls and each one of my grandchildren came to spend time with me, which was so special. When your life changes so dramatically from being with someone you love for fifty-four years to suddenly being on your own, you can do two things. You can get back up on that bike and carry on, or you sit in your sadness and wallow. I knew Ted was tucked up safely with Jesus, so my life had to go on, and I do more now for God as I am more available. It took a while of finding myself again, but I was always trusting God in everything and speaking to Him daily. I tend to speak to Him and pray in my garden as I feel so close to Him there with the birds singing. For twenty years now, I have talked to Him in my garden; it's one of my favourite places to be alone with Him. I had a conservatory built on my home, as it was something that Ted and I were going to do. I sit in there and pray. I call it my prayer room, a lot of prayers and declarations go on in there, and people who visit say it is so peaceful.

I spend a lot more time praying now and more time studying the Word. At one time, I thought I was too old to do anything, but God told me different. He told me,

"You have a Ministry that comes from the heart. People feel close to Me when they are with you. They feel My presence even if they don't know Me. They feel calm and at ease with you because you walk with Me. Keep on being who you are,

you are important to Me, you are special to Me. I can trust you with your loyalty and love for Me. You never fail Me!"

What a beautiful love letter from my wonderful Father. If you are reading this and you have not made Jesus your Lord and Saviour, please do not let the chance go by. I had a saying that I had given me and it is so true. Some people miss heaven by 18 inches, the distance between their heads, and their hearts. One of the devil's most successful wiles is 'Wait a while'. We need to listen to God, don't delay any more, and say this prayer now.

Dear Jesus, please forgive me, I have sinned against you, and I ask you now to please forgive me and come into my life and make me part of your family. I repent of my sins, and I need you as my Lord and Saviour, and I ask that you will now be my Lord and lead me and guide me. Baptise me with your Holy Spirit, and I place myself into your Hands. Amen.

As I got to the end of writing this book, I heard a song by Zach Williams and Dolly Parton called, 'There was Jesus'. I felt so much for this song, as it was almost like it was my life. Each time I was alone, rejected, and abandoned, Jesus was there holding on to me with those arms. There were many more times when I leaned on Him, and there was Jesus. He alone, has everything in His Hands, and what a safe place to be.

"These are just some of my promises that I say out loud over me, and my family. For by your words, you will be justified, and by your words you will be condemned." **(Matthew 12:37)**

Stand therefore until you get what you are standing for. If you are willing to stand, forever you won't be standing for long.

"So shall My Word be that goes forth from My mouth. It shall not return to Me void, but it shall accomplish what I please, and it shall prosper in the thing for which I sent it." **(Isaiah 55:11)**

"For the Word of God is living and powerful and sharper than any two-edged

sword piecing even to the division of soul and spirit and of joints and marrow and is a discerner of the thoughts and intents of the heart." **(Hebrews 4:12)**

"The word of our God stands for ever and I stand on the Word. The just will live by faith, I expect what I say with my mouth to come to pass. I have access to the throne I am righteous in right standing with God. I walk by faith I act on the word of God I declare what I believe with my mouth My confidence is in Him. God watches over His Word to perform it and I stay with the word of God. My words abide in you and My words will never pass away. I act on the word of God to get results. Man lives by every word that proceeds out of the mouth of God." **(Isaiah 40:8)**

"This book of the law shall not depart from your mouth, but you shall meditate in it day and night that you may observe to do according to all that is written in it. For then you will make your way prosperous and then you will have good success. Be strong and of good courage, do not be afraid or be dismayed, for the Lord is with you wherever you go." **(Joshua 1:8-9)**

"As for Me says the Lord, this is My covenant with them. My Spirit who is upon you, and My Words which I have put in your mouth, shall not depart from your mouth, nor from the mouth of your descendants from this time and forever more." **(Isaiah 59:21)**

"He shall call upon Me and I will answer him, I will be with him in trouble and I will deliver him and honour him. With long life I will satisfy him. For He shall give His angels charge over you, to keep you in all your ways." **(Psalm 91)**

"And if you are Christs then you are Abraham's seed and heirs according to the promise. Heavenly Father I attend to your Word, I incline my ears to your sayings. I will not let them depart from mine eyes; I keep them in the midst of my heart for they are life and healing to all my flesh. These are the healing scriptures I speak over me and my family" **(Galations 3:29)**

"He sent forth His Word and healed me." **(Psalm 107:20)**

*"You have given me abundant life. I receive that life through your Word, and it flows to every organ of my body bringing healing and health." **(John 10:10) and (John 6:63)***

*"God sent His word and healed them." **(Psalm 107:20)***

*"It is the Spirit who gives life the flesh profits nothing, the Words that I speak to you are Spirit and they are life." **(John 6:63)***

This is why I speak these declarations, they are life. The word of God is alive. I refuse to let sickness dominate my body as I am redeemed from the curse. The life of God flows with me, bringing healing to every fibre of my being. Body, I speak the word of faith to you. I demand that every internal organ performs a perfect work, for you are the temple of the Holy Spirit, therefore I charge you in the name of Jesus Christ to be healed and made whole in Jesus Name.

Faith is my servant, and I release it to bring forth a miracle in the mighty name of Jesus. I stand on the word and I bring the word to pass. I have an abundance of the anointing of God. I believe that all my needs are met. I believe I am healed from the top of my head to the soles of my feet. Praise God.

I speak (Psalm 91) over my family, and I plead the precious blood of Jesus over them. Do not stop speaking the Word of God over your situations.

*"And My God shall supply all your needs according to His riches in Glory by Christ Jesus." **(Philippians 4:19)***

*"My heart stands in awe of your Word, I rejoice at Your Word, as one who finds great treasure." **(Psalm 119:161-162)***

What a wonderful treasure it is!

www.ingramcontent.com/pod-product-compliance
Lightning Source LLC
Chambersburg PA
CBHW071542080526
44588CB00011B/1757